I0430151

Mind Control

Secrets of the Subconscious Mind

Eleanor Price

Disclaimer: All attempts have been made by the author to provide factual and accurate content. No responsibility will be taken by the author or publisher for any damages caused by misuse of the content described in this book. The content of this book has been derived from various sources. Please consult an expert before attempting anything described in this book.

TABLE OF CONTENTS

INTRODUCTION

I am writing this book to introduce the idea of mind control to everyone. I want people to understand that it really is possible to use mind control on those around you and it is possible for those around you to use mind control on you. I am writing this because I want those who are using mind control to understand how it really works and for those who are being controlled to understand that they can break free of mind control. There are benefits to using mind control and I will discuss them in this book. If you are interested in using mind control, I feel that it is very important for you to have the best information available.

With that in mind, I spent days searching for as much information as I could find to pass on to you the reader about using mind control. Please be forewarned using mind control on anyone is not a game, it is very serious and should be treated as such. Please read through the entire eBook before attempting any form of mind control. You will learn what mind control is, how it works and how to use it in your everyday life.

You will also learn how you can benefit from learning how to use mind control as well as how to know if someone is using mind control techniques on you. There are warnings in the final chapter that you must know before trying to perform mind control.

Above all, I thank you for downloading and taking the time to read my book and I truly hope that you enjoy it.

Thanks, I hope you enjoy it!

CHAPTER 1

What is Mind Control?

Mind control is the method used to control the mind of a human and influence control over the actions of said person. Mind control is also referred to as brain washing, thought control, coercive persuasion. It results in the inability to think independently or have any control over behavior, emotions, and actions. Many people think that mind control is when a person uses cunning methods to coerce others to conform to the wishes of the one who is manipulating them. Although using cunning methods is part of using mind control, it does not always have to be about manipulation. People also perceive mind control as something that is bad and is only used by bad people. This is another false perception. Mind control is only bad if it takes advantage of the person it is being used on, but the fact is that you cannot make someone do something that they are morally or ethically against doing. For instance, you cannot make someone who believes that murder is wrong commit murder. Mind control can be used to bring out the worst in people as well as the best in people, it all depends on the person who controlling the mind of someone.

Thought reform is actually learning how to change people's minds and behaviors. Influencing the way people think is not negative. All of us influence the way people think on a daily basis, using mind control is simply taking control of that influence and using it for your own benefit. When you watch television ads you are being subjected to coercive persuasion you told multiple times how happy the product on television will make you and how you must have it. Those who are easily coerced are convinced that they cannot live without the product advertised on the television. Think about it like this, has your child ever been watching television and an ad come on of the newest toy available? While watching the ad the child becomes almost hypnotized by it and when it is over the child is convinced that they must have the toy! They will tell you that they won't have any friends if you don't buy it for them or they will never be happy without that particular toy. Coercive persuasion has been used on them. It was not unethical nor was it someone trying to manipulate the child in a negative way, it was simply and ad that was trying to sell a product.

Mind control is not about turning people into zombies to do what you wish at your will, it is simply about influencing the way they think in order to get what you want.

Today, mind control has nothing to do with magic powers or mysterious arts, it is simply about marketing. Many people are put off by the thought of mind control, thinking that it causes people to do crazy things but the fact is that the everyday person can use coercive persuasion to alter someone's thoughts and get them to do what they want.

Mind control has been used by many governments on its citizens for things such as terrorist attacks, assassinations, and mass shootings just to name a few but that kind of mind control takes years to learn and it is done by way of torture, electric impulses, strict regimes, and many other unethical practices. That is not the type of mind control that you can use in your life on a daily basis.

There also have been cases where using certain drugs or heavily medicating a person can enable someone to control the mind of another. Physical, emotional, and mental abuse are also forms of mind control. Have you ever known a woman who was suffering from physical, emotional, or mental abuse? Have you noticed that she will jump at the chance to make here partner happy? Even though she is being tormented, and tortured, she does everything she can to try and do better. This technique of mind control being used is a very popular one. It is where the person manipulating will withhold love from the one who is being manipulated. They may also physically torture the person causing a mental break. The person they are manipulating will become reliant on them to make all of their decisions for them and they will do anything to receive any form of love from the manipulator.

That is not the type of mind control you will learn in this book. For this book we are going to stick to controlling the mind of others through influence and getting what you want through persuasive coercion. There is no need to torture someone in order for you to get them to do what you want them to do.

Who Can You Use Mind Control On?

The short answer is anyone is susceptible to mind control, but there are those who are more vulnerable than others. Here is a list of traits that make people more vulnerable to mind control.

✓ Those who do not understand how mind control works,

✓ Those who have the mentality that "it will never happen to me",

✓ Those who think everyone is basically good,

✓ Those who do not want to believe that there are evil people in this world.,

✓ Those who have low self-esteem,

✓ Those who are facing a stressful situation such as the loss of a job or relationship,

✓ Those who feel alone,

✓ Those who are dissatisfied with life,

✓ Those who have the desire to take care of others,

✓ Those who have a high regard for authority,

✓ Those who are seeking spirituality,

✓ Those who are suffering from some form of anxiety or depression,

✓ Those who are addicted to drugs or alcohol,

✓ Those who are preoccupied with what others think about them.

There are there factors that will matter when you are trying to learn and use mind control. The first factor is called your private personality, this is who you truly are. Your thoughts, feelings, hopes, and values. These may be things that you do not share with those around you. The second factor is your public self, this is how you behave around people, this is what you share with those around you. It is usually your most positive features. Finally your reputation will be the last factor that will play a part in your ability to use mind control. If you are perceived as a person who cannot be trusted or a person that others do not feel comfortable around than you will not be able to use mind control on those around you. On the other hand, if you are perceived as someone who is very trust worthy and everyone is able to relax when they are around you, mind control will be very easy for you.

Mind control is all about power. It is about having the power over others in order to get them to do what you want them to do. It does not matter if it is getting them to give you a big raise or if you are trying to get them to buy your product, it is all about having the power over their mind in order to get them to do so.

Many people think that parents use mind control on their children when they are trying to raise them with social, moral, cultural and personal standards. They feel that in a way the parents are influencing the child's mind to become exactly what the parents want them to be. It is also a common belief that the military uses mind control on its recruits when they are submitted to techniques that belittle or demoralize them in order to break down their personal ego and build up the idea of group identification.

Many also believe that when a person is taken captive and they begin to feel compassion for their captor that they are a victim of mind control. Some people also believe that subliminal messages in television ads and programming is a form of mind control.

In Haiti, people are made into living zombies and forced to work as slaves on farms given drugs that allow their master to use mind control on them. Very few of these people ever rebel against their masters and even fewer ever escape their bondage.

In this book, I simply want to discuss the types of mind control you can use on a daily basis in order to get what you want from those around you. When it comes to the ethics of mind control, it is up to each individual person to determine how far they will take using mind control and if the benefits outweigh the risks.

Mind Control

CHAPTER 2

How Does Mind Control Work?

When you use mind control on a person, they are not even aware of what is happening, and when they reach a decision, they think they have done it completely of their own free will. They have actually reached the decision on their own, but with the help of your influence.

When you master mind control, you will be able to influence those around you, plant seeds of suggestion in their minds, and get them to do what you want them to do. Whether it is buying a product that you are selling or simply completing a task that you want them to complete, you will be able to influence them to do so.

Mind control works like this...

First the person has to be in a relaxed state, you will not be able to control someone's mind if they are not relaxed. After the person is relaxed, you will be able to use the techniques that you will learn later on in the book on them. You will also learn how to get people to relax around you.

You can use mind control online in a blog post or in social media. Take this for example:

If I wanted you to buy something for instance, if I was selling my car, but I knew you were not really interested so I changed the subject to my new book I am writing. Now look back on the paragraph you just read, what do you find? If I had not told you to look back on the paragraph you would have had no idea what I did but you realize that the words "buy my book now" are all in bold. These four words will stand out in your mind even if you do not consciously know it, causing you to think that you should buy my book. You can use this for all sorts of things when it comes to social media or internet marketing.

When using mind control on someone, you want to make sure that you do all of the thinking for them, do not tell them that they should think it over. The techniques will be discussed in later chapters, but the way it works is that by doing all of the thinking for them you are able to make them believe whatever it is that you want them to.

Mind control works by convincing someone to do something that they have no ethical or moral problems with doing. For instance, let's say you are going to buy a house and you want the seller to drop the price by 25,000 dollars. You can use mind control to get them to do so. On the other hand, you cannot use mind control to get them to give you the house for free. This would go against their wants and needs.

The fact is that you cannot use mind control to get someone to do what they really are not open to doing in the first place.

When using mind control there are a few things that you have to do first in order to prepare the person. First, you must make the person perceive that you like them that you genuinely have an interest in them and you are concerned about what is important to them. Everyone wants to be liked, noticed, an accepted, when you compliment people and show them that you accept who they are, you are using a very powerful method of getting them to like you. Then you need to make them think that you are just like them. Many times the manipulator will talk about things that have happened to them in their lives that relate to the things that have happened to the "victim". Even making up things so that the person feels as if the manipulator is letting their guard down and opening up to them. This is a great step toward strengthening the bond between the "victim" and manipulator. After you have gotten the person to like you, you will have to convince them that their secrets are safe with you. Because you are sharing intimate details about your life (even if they are not true) with the victim it becomes much easier for them to let their guard down and discuss their personal issues with you. This can take a little bit of time but most people will open up fairly quickly. Finally you will have to make them believe that you are the perfect lover, friend, or companion for them. You will make them believe that you accept them for who they are and that there is nothing you would change about them. You highlight the things that the two of you have in common and build a strong reputation for yourself in the mind of the "victim". They will begin to believe that your relationship is different and special in some way.

This will open them up to trusting you and feeling comfortable enough around you that you will be able to use mind control on them. It all depends on how you are perceived by the person you are trying to use mind control on. The trick of mind control is making the "victim" think that the one doing the controlling is a friend and someone who has their best interests at heart. This will cause the person being manipulated to actually be a willing participant because they feel like they are being helped in some way and they think that they are making their own decisions.

All of this is normal for building a relationship, the only difference is that you as the manipulator are not interested in building a relationship with the person and are only interested with what you can gain. This relationship is a false one that is usually built on lies. Another reason why this is not a normal relationship is because it does not last once you as the manipulator have reached your desired outcome for the relationship, it is pushed aside and forgotten about therefore the manipulator has no further use for the person and discards them.

When you begin using mind control, you want to make sure that you start off small. This means that you are to start off with a small request something that is easy for the person that you are using mind control on to do. You do not want to start out by asking someone for a large sum of money or for them to do a huge favor for you. You will be able to do this later when you have developed your skills further but in the beginning keep your requests small and easy to perform.

Mind control works by planting small seeds into the person's subconscious. These seeds will begin to grow over time and you will be able to control more and more of the person's thoughts, behaviors, and actions. You will also be able to cause a loss of memory, or cause someone to desire something.

Mind control works in the same way that social influence works, this is when you are continually influenced by those around you, it shapes who you are in the moment and who you will become in the future. Social influence is what determines what brands are popular, how people talk, and how people act. Social influence is very similar to mind control but mind control is a very invasive form of influence so it requires the subject to be dependent on the person who is trying to control them. This is why it is so successfully used on people who do not have many friends, people who are going through a divorce, or who have been recently divorced, and those who are leaving home for the first time in their lives. These people do not have many if any other people to turn to they become dependent on the person who is trying to control them.

Much like social influence, mind control must be used each and every day on the subject. You have to ensure that they must believe that the controller is the only person they can turn to and the only person that they can trust. Being in constant contact with the subject will allow the controller to gain more and more control over the subject, and as each day passes the subject will become more and more dependent on the controller.

There are four basic steps that have to be taken when trying to control someone's mind. The first thing that you have to do is identify your target. Once you have identified your target you must make sure they become aware of you. This is called the physical layer of mind control. So you will request their attention by placing yourself close to them, they will grant you the attention that you are asking for and then you will gain access to them. After you have gained access, you can more on to the logical layer of mind control. This is where you use the attention you have gained in order to feed them information. You discuss what it is you want and why. The next layer of mind control is the emotional layer. In this step you cause your subject to have an emotional response to what it is you are telling them, without allowing yourself to be sucked into their emotions. You must play the part and pretend to have the correct emotional responses but not allow your emotions to become part of the situation. The final layer is called the hyper-arousal layer. This is where the fight or flight response kicks in on the subject. You can use something to make them feel vulnerable. For example, if I were a cult leader, I would start out by getting the persons attention, telling them about all that I believe in, get them to become emotionally involved in what I am telling them, and then tell them if they do not join me the will suffer some severe consequence. It is that simple.

CHAPTER 3

What are the Benefits of Mind Control?

Using mind control on those around you can have many benefits. You can learn how to make more sales by using mind control, get people to do whatever you want them to do, get people to give things to you, and even control how people feel about you.

By using mind control, you may be able to do things for you for free that would normally cost you money. You can get people to believe in what you say and even share it with others.

I recently watched a video online that talked about mind control, and it asked questions such as:

- Do you want a large amount of followers?
- Do you want to be treated like a god?
- Do you want people to give you all of their worldly possessions?
- Do you want people to do whatever you ask without questioning you?

- Do you want people to do whatever it takes to make you happy?
- Would you like it if people would kill for you?

Now some of these questions seem a little outrageous, not everyone who is interested in mind control is a cult leader in the making, they don't want people who will kill for them, and they don't want people to freely give them all of their worldly possessions. Most of the people who are interested in using mind control are normal people who want to learn how to use mind control in order to benefit themselves or those around them.

Ways you can benefit from using mind control:

- Get the promotion you have been asking for – you have worked for it now get what you deserve.

- Get people to buy your product or service-tapping into the market can be hard, use mind control to ensure your business is successful.

- Get people to do things for you. Keeping up with life can be hard at times. Sometimes we need a little help and we don't like paying for it, so just use mind control to get people to help you pick up the slack. Need your lawn mowed? Use mind control to get someone to do it for you.

- Get your children to mind! Yes you can even use mind control on your children to help mold them into the people that you want them to be. Can't get your kids to clean their rooms? Use mind control to get them to do whatever it is you ask of them.

- Use mind control to bring your ex back. Many of us have heard that you can't make someone love you, well guess what, that is wrong. By using mind control you can bring your ex back and make them love you.

- Get out of trouble. Next time you find yourself getting pulled over for speeding simply use mind control to get yourself out of the ticket.

As you can see, using mind control can benefit you in many ways. As long as you are not using unethical techniques such as torture or sleep deprivation to get what you want.

The benefits of using mind control over those around you are basically being able to get whatever you want from whom ever you want whenever you want it.

How you can use mind control to benefit those around you:

Did you know that by using mind control you can help those around you? For example, do you know anyone who is really smart but just can't get it together because of some mental block? Did you know that through mind control you can take that block away and allow them to really be their true self?

For example, you have a friend who is very artistic, but because of their low self-confidence they do not show many people their paintings. You can use mind control on the person to make them open up and display their paintings, you can help them sell their art by using mind control on them. If you were to use mind control in this situation, then you have just helped your friend become successful by using mind control on them.

Helping those around you is the greatest benefit to using mind control. Helping them to become what they truly want to be without causing harm to them is what mind control is all about. This is the part of mind control that most people do not understand. When people think about mind control they think about causing others harm, not about bringing peace and joy to the lives of others.

The cons of using mind control:

You may look at the benefit of being able to get people to do whatever you want, whenever you want and think that it would be wonderful, but before ever trying anything new you must not only look at the pros, but you must also look at the cons.

- It may be tempting to abuse the power that you have when you are using mind control. If you are the kind of person who knows that they will continue to take and take until there is nothing left there is a high chance that you will abuse your power. Also, if you are a person who has a history of abusing power that has been given to them than you may want to reconsider using mind control on anyone.

- You can become suspicious of everyone around you. When you begin using mind control techniques, there is a chance that you will be unable to trust anyone in your own life for fear that they are using the same techniques on you. You will find it harder to make friends with new people and can very easily become isolated.

- Using mind control can come back to haunt you. If those around you find out that you are using mind control techniques you may be left with no one in your life. Think about how you would feel if you found out that one of your friends was using mind control, even if it was not on you. Would you ever be able to trust that person again? Would you want to continue allowing that person to be part of your life?

- If you become angry at the person you are using mind control on what will you do? Using mind control takes a lot of discipline and wisdom. You cannot allow yourself to cause harm to someone while using mind control just because you are upset with them at that time.

- You may become obsessed with using mind control and lose your own identity along the way. Many people become so power hungry when they use mind control that they do not think about the person that they are becoming until it is too late. They are only thinking about what they can gain. Then when they realize what they have become it seems far too late to ever go back to the person that they once were.

- The final con that you have to think about is if using mind control on someone goes against your moral or ethical beliefs. Do you feel that you have the right to decide for someone what actions they will take in their own lives?

Mind control is something that has many benefits if it is used properly but it is also something that has been abused by many people. I has caused harm to thousands of people and to their families all around the world. If you really want to benefit from using mind control than you have to be able to ensure that you do not lose control of yourself. You have to focus on getting what you want without taking advantage of your subjects, and you have to ensure that you do not allow mind control to take you over. It is a personal decision to use mind control but it is not a decision that should be taken lightly. You should spend time weighing the pros and cons, think about how you will ensure that you do not become a victim of mind control by allowing it to take over your life, and seriously think about if you could become one of those people who ends up abusing the power that comes along with being able to use mind control.

If you feel that you can handle all of the power that comes with using mind control and you will be able to keep control of yourself when using it than you should continue on, but if you think that there is even the slightest chance that you could cause harm to those around you by using mind control, you need to stop now and do some self-work before continuing on and beginning to use mind control.

If it is all about trying to get a group of people to follow or worship you than the techniques that are taught in this book are not for you. On the other hand, if you want to use mind control in order to help yourself or those around you than you will learn all you need to in the following chapters. Mind control is not always about getting people to drink the purple Kool-Aid, it can be about helping them get what they really want and helping you be successful in life.

CHAPTER 4

Beginner Techniques

In this chapter I want to discuss beginner's techniques for using mind control. As I discussed earlier, you have to ensure that the person you are trying to use mind control on trusts you and feels relaxed around you. After you have accomplished this you may then begin using the techniques I will discuss in this chapter.

Let's start with how you use your voice. When most people talk, they finish a sentence by using a higher pitched tone than what they normally talk in. If you want to persuade someone to do what you want them to do, when you talk to them you should finish each sentence with a lower tone that what you were stating the rest of the sentence in. This gives their brain the impression that you are demanding them to do what you are asking of them. When you use a higher tone at the end of a sentence the brain instead perceives it as a question. So if you are "asking" someone if they would buy your product or whatever you are wanting of them and you finish the sentence with a lower tone of your voice, they still think you are asking a question but the subconscious mind takes it as a demand. This changes the way people think about the "question" you asked them. Using a lower tone at the end of your sentences will cause the person to do whatever it is that you are asking of them. You should practice this before you use it because when you naturally speak, you use a higher tone at the end of the sentence and if you try to chance this while speaking to a person and don't practice it, it will sound awkward and will not work.

The next thing you need to think about is what you are saying. You need to use terms that get the brain working. Using terms such as "what if", "think about", "what would happen" these will open up the persons mind to your suggestions and will allow you to tell them why they should do what you are asking of them.

When you are getting to know the person, they will reveal all of their secrets to you, then when you begin using mind control on them you are in a sense going to use it against them. For example if the person confides in you that they only buy certain things because they love the way others look at them when they see them with that specific product. They have confided in you what makes them feel good. So if you are trying to sell them something, you can say something like, "Imagine how jealous all those people will be that do not have the chance to get this, think about how they will look at you and wish they were you."

This makes the person you are trying to use mind control on think about how good it feels to them when others look at the things they have, they enjoy making others jealous and you are using that to sell your product. This is called anchoring, which means simply that you take the memories of good feelings and project them on to whatever it is that you want the person to do. You have anchored their mind to the good feelings they had and projecting them onto your product.

You can also use sexual attraction to help use mind control on those around you. The way this works it that you build up a lot of sexual tension between you and the person you want to control. You make them think that they will have the chance to be with you. They will get to a point where they feel like they are "falling in love" with you and this is where you can begin to control them using other techniques. This makes mind control very easy on these people because they already want to do whatever they can do please you.

When you use this technique, you want to keep the person sexually aroused but not give into them. You want to withhold yourself from them so that they will do whatever it is you want them to thinking that they will in turn get to have some type of physical contact with you.

Pacing is the next beginner's technique that I would like to talk about. This is where you hypnotize someone during everyday conversation by mirroring their actions, body language, and the way they talk. You want to make sure that you do not do it in a way that is apparent to them but in a way that only the subconscious mind picks up on.   This will once again cause them to trust you and make them think that you are just like them. They will become attracted to you as a person because they will see themselves in you.

After you have become successful at mirroring their actions, you will begin the process of bring them to an altered state of consciousness. In order to do this you will need them to relax and breathe deeply, you can accomplish this by having them tell you a story about a happy relaxing time in their life. They do not have to reach a deep hypnotic trance in order for you to complete the hypnosis, as long as they are in a relaxed state it will work.

Now it is time to place the command into your conversation. For instance if the command is <u>clean your room</u> you would want to incorporate this into a sentence or question. You can start with asking them how often they clean their room, then you will need to keep adding a few layers to it. Ask things like, how do you feel after you <u>clean your room,</u> do you feel better when you <u>clean your room,</u> and so on. Now this may seem very simple but it is best to work with a simple command when starting out than to work with something more complex. You will work up to the more complex demands later. You want to make sure that you repeat the phrase <u>clean your room</u> multiple times while still keeping the person in a relaxed state.

When you begin practicing this, you want to make sure that whatever your command is can be carried out immediately. There is no point in using mind control on someone if they cannot do the action you are requesting right then. If you use pacing, you will see that after your conversation the person has the urge to go and do what you wanted them to do.

Repetition is very important when it comes to using mind control on someone, first you must be very patient and remain calm at all times. You do not want to become over baring and become angry with the person because the mind control is working slower than you would like it to. You will find that this is one of the easiest methods of mind control. The more that you repeat something, the higher the chances of you obtaining it. This does not mean that you continually repeat the same words or phrases over and over, this will only annoy the people around you. You simply discuss it in different ways over a period of time. When you repeat yourself, you cause a hypnotic impact on the mind.

So let's go back to the idea that you want your child to clean their room. You will repeat this multiple times throughout the day using terms such as: You need to clean your room. When are you going to clean your room? I need you to clean your room. Clean your room. How long until you go clean your room? You will continue doing this until it is in the child's mind that they need to go clean their room that they cannot think of anything else until they have cleaned their room.

Make the person you are using mind control on perceive you as figure of authority. You can do this by using the fact that you are successful at your job, or that you have a degree, or just by using the way you dress to cause them to perceive you as an authority figure. People are often subconsciously intimidated by authority and they are more willing to do what those who are in a position of authority want them to do. This is why you see so many people following cult leaders, the person has convinced them that they are in a position of authority and people naturally want to please those that hold those positions.

The last technique I want to talk about in this chapter is giving a reason. Give the person you are trying to use mind control on a reason that they should do what you are asking. When you give people a reason, they are much more inclined to do what you need them to do. For example, if you need someone to mow your lawn and you are talking the person you want to use mind control on, you can say something like, "I really need someone to mow my lawn for me because I am so busy with the kids, work, and my job that I barely have time to sleep. It would help me so much if I could find someone to mow my lawn." This has given them a reason which is to help you because you are overwhelmed with all that you have to do. This is a very effective technique and I can tell you from firsthand experience it works very well. It can pretty much be used on anyone in your life, not just someone you are focusing on using mind control on. It can be used on family and friends also and they have no idea that you used the technique to get them to do what you wanted them to do.

CHAPTER 5

Advanced Techniques

In this chapter I want to discuss advanced techniques that you can utilize when using mind control. First I would like to state that it is very important that you master the techniques mentioned in the previous chapter before attempting to use any of the techniques given in this chapter. It is important that you work through each and every technique that I have already given you so that you can use the techniques I give you in this chapter to build upon your mind control skills.

First I would like to discuss the silent treatment as an advanced technique in mind control. This one may seem childish on the surface but if you look deeper it is a great technique that you can use in order to control the way someone thinks and feels. As discussed earlier when you want to control someone's mind, you want to make them feel as if they can be relaxed around you and you want them to become dependent on your friendship. Using the silent treatment may seem like it is counter intuitive but this is how it works. Once the person depends on you, they feel as if they must be in contact with you, they rely on communication with you and they may feel as if they are falling in love with you. Now if you want them to do something for you, you take that away from them. You suddenly ignore them, don't answer their texts for a day and see what happens! After you ignore them for a little while and I do stress little while, you pick up as if nothing happened. The subject will be so grateful that you are back in their life that they will do almost anything you ask of them. I stressed a little while because you don't want this to go on too long, you want them to remain in the frame of mind that they are unable to function without you being part of their life. I would not continue the silent treatment for longer than a twenty- four hour period.

Using cause and effect to control the minds of others. This one is also fairly simple but it takes a lot of prac-tice to learn how to talk in a cause and effect manner. Let's go back to the clean your room scenario, when you use cause and effect, you will say to the subject, "You can't find your shoes (this is the cause) so you might want to clean your room."(This is the effect) Simply stating cause and effect to someone makes the feel like you are right and that they should heed your suggestion. This is just a basic example. A more manipulative and complex way to use cause and effect to control someone's mind would be if you are trying to sell your product, you could say, "It is obvious that you are an intelligent person, therefore you can understand all of the benefits that come along with the purchase of this product." The cause is that the person is intelligent, and the effect is that they understand all of the benefits they will receive. Using this in your everyday talk will ensure that you are able to use mind control to get what you want from people.

Using reverse phycology in order to control someone's mind. Many people are confused when it comes to using reverse phycology, instead of using reverse phycology, they become more of a passive aggressive. They will say something like, "I don't care if you go out with your buddies," thinking that it will stop the person from going out with their friends. In reality this does not work, it is just a way to annoy most people and you will never get anyone to do what you want if you are passive aggressive.

So let's go back to needing someone to mow your lawn. You can always say to your husband, "Hey are you going to mow the lawn?" Or you can use reverse phycology and say, "The lawn is in serious need of being mowed, so I have decided to hire a lawn service. I need you to give me money to pay them."

Watch your husband jump up and mow the lawn! What this does is provides an alternative action to your husband mowing the lawn without placing any blame on him for not having it mowed. The alternative should not be one that the person would normally agree with, for this example paying for a lawn service when your husband can cut it himself. So rather than your husband being preoccupied because you are placing blame on him for not mowing the lawn all he can do is consider how much it is going to cost to hire a lawn service and how it would just be cheaper if he did it himself. This is what makes reverse phycology affective, as long as you say it like you mean it.

Staying positive is another advanced technique when it comes to using mind control. People respond better to positive motivation than they do to negative stimulation. For example, instead of threatening and yelling at someone to do what it is that you want them to do, you should reinforce the positive benefits that they will receive if they do what you want. You have to continually make them think that you have their best interest at heart and that you are simply suggesting they do what is best for them. It works in much the same way as using rewards and punishment. People will respond better to receiving a reward for a job well done than they will to being punished for not doing their best. They will work hard in order to receive the reward you are offering. The reward when it comes to mind control is to make you happy.

Planting seeds of thought. This is one of the most subtle ways you can use mind control to get people to do what you want. Take for example if you are trying to get a friend to be healthier but the problem is they are addicted to hamburgers. You can't just come out and tell them all the things that are wrong with fast food and restaurant burgers this will just get on their nerves, but you can take a more subtle approach. Next time you go out to eat with your friend and you are looking through the menu, make sure you point out how you are looking for something besides a burger because of the news report you saw about how it was processed. Next time you are not feeling well joke around that you think you are getting mad cow disease. Once you have dropped enough seeds of thought into your friends mind, they will not be able to avoid thinking about how unhealthy burgers can be for them.

Asking for more is a great advanced technique when it comes to using mind control. You may think to yourself, "How am I going to get what I want by asking for more?" The answer is simple. Let's say you are trying to get someone to donate 10 dollars to your cause, this may be a large sum of money for that person. So you will begin by telling them that most people are donating at least 25 dollars. The person doesn't want to give you 25 dollars so you tell them that you can settle for a donation of 10 dollars. This will make the person feel relieved that you are not asking them for the full 25 dollars and they will gladly hand over the 10 dollars. I have used this technique in my own life and was able to get 800 dollars out of someone. It simply went like this, I needed 1500 dollars, I called the person on the phone and explained to them why I needed the 1500 dollars. They of course said they would love to help but 1500 was just too much I then informed them that someone else had offered to give me 600 dollars and if they could only come up with the other 800 dollars then I would have what I needed. Guess what, within an hour they were at my house delivering the 800 dollars I actually needed. The idea of giving me 1500 dollars was something they could not wrap their mind around but when I dropped that amount to almost half they were more than willing to bring it to me. That is what you have to do. You need to at least ask for double what you need and then when you drop the sum, they will be more than happy to help you out.

Reframing can be used in order to control someone's mind. This is used when someone tries to give you an excuse of why they cannot do what you are asking of them. For instance, if you want someone to go out and jog with you but their excuse for not wanting to go is that it is hot. You will state their excuse in your reply to them. For example, you could say, "It is a little warm out but that will only cause us to sweat a little more which will only cause us to lose more weight!" You have to put a positive spin on their excuse and show the person how they will benefit from what they are trying to use as an excuse.

Use what motivates the subject to get them to do what you want. For example, if your subject wants to be popular and date the most attractive people than you will be able to use that against them to sell almost any type of diet, exercise program, or drug. The way you do this is that you talk about how they will be able to reach their goals of being popular and dating only the most attractive people if they buy your product. You say things like, "Imagine what it would be like to walk up to the most beautiful woman in the room knowing that she would walk out on your arm." You will make them think about how happy they would be if they bought your product.

Finally, if you are working with your subject on a day to day basis, you will be able to use several of these techniques at on time. Using more than one technique will give you better results than just using one technique at a time. You can use a few basic and a few advanced techniques at the same time on the same subject. I do advise that you learn each and every technique before you begin using multiple techniques. Take a week or two and spend it focusing on each technique this will ensure that you are successful at using mind control on your subjects.

CHAPTER 6

Is Someone Using Mind Control on You?

Learning how to use mind control may make you begin to wonder if you could be a victim of mind control. Maybe you have noticed a few similarities in the techniques I have described and one of your relationships. If you think you are a subject of mind control, ask yourself the following questions:

1. Is there one person in your life that you seem to continually do things for?- If you find that there is one person in your life that you can just not seem to say no to no matter what they ask of you than you may be a victim of mind control.

2. Why do you continue to do things for this one person? Is it because you feel obligated or are you just trying to be nice?- Being nice to a person is one thing but if you feel like you "have" to do whatever it is this person is

asking of you, chances are that you are a subject of mind control.

3.   Is there any benefit to you for having the relationship that you feel could involve mind control? - Is the other person the only one who is benefitting from the relationship? Do you find that you seem to always be running around trying to make the other person happy and give them the things they desire but you are getting no benefits yourself? This is a huge sign that you are the subject of mind control.

4.   How would you feel if this person suddenly disappeared from your life? – If you would feel as though your entire world is falling apart than you are probably being controlled. This is different than a husband/wife relationship. This is someone who is not married to you but seems to be the center of your entire life.

5.   Does this person disappear or ignore you when you do not give into their wants? This is the technique called the silent treatment, they are trying to show you how hard your life would be without them and they are forc-

ing you to do whatever they want in order to keep them in your life.

If you think that you are a victim of mind control, there are things that you can do in order to break free. You have already started by realizing that there is a chance someone is using mind control to get what they want from you. Here are some things you can do in order to break free of mind control.

✓ Interact and connect with others on a regular basis. This is the next step you must take if you want to break free from being a victim of mind control. This is because you have to realize that there are other people out there who do want to be your friend, there really are people who will be sincere and who will genuinely care about you without trying to control you.

✓ If you find that your mind is constantly being bombarded with thoughts that are disturbing to you and you feel have been planted by a person who is using mind control, you have to find a way to distract yourself from those thoughts. You need to find a way to keep busy and allow your mind to think for itself. When you begin to think about one of these thoughts, you need to immediately force yourself to think about something else.

✓ Do not entertain the thought that you are evil. This is just one more way that you will become susceptible to mind control. It may also be a seed that was planted in your mind in order to ensure that you comply with the demands of the person who is using mind control on you. Remind yourself that you are a loving and wonderful person whenever these thoughts enter you mind.

✓ Don't allow fear to stop you from making new friends. The person who is controlling your mind may have said things like, "No one else will ever care about you like I do," or, "You don't deserve to have friends." You have to put these thoughts out of your head no matter how hard it is and allow yourself to meet new people. Remind yourself that they only said those things because they wanted to keep you for themselves, you are such a wonderful person that they did not want to share you with anyone else.

✓ Don't worry about what others think of you, when you are around people do everything you can to be yourself and know that they will love you for who you are. When you are alone, you may have to battle with the thoughts that have been planted in your mind but you should be able to be yourself around others.

✓ Do not think that all humans are evil, evil is something that is learned and not something people are born with. You now know that there are people out there who are bad and who will try to control you, you can look for the warning signs now but you must understand not everyone is like that.

✓ Avoid alcohol and drugs, will only make it easier for you to be controlled. You need to avoid them at least until you break free of the controller in your life. You may choose to avoid them all together afterwards so you never go through this experience again but that is a personal choice.

✓ Find a good psychiatrist in order to avoid long lasting damage. You should find a good psychiatrist that you can talk to about the experience. Another alternative to this is to write a book or find a support group for people who have been through being a victim of mind control.

How can you know if you have joined a group that is using mind control? The questions that I am going to have you ask yourself are not limited to religious groups, there are many other types of groups that can and do use mind control on a regular basis so you should ask yourself the following questions to determine if in fact you have joined a group of people who may be using mind control.

1. Do you feel that no matter how hard you try, what you do is not good enough for the leader or the group? Making you feel like trying your best is a way that the groups will try to break you down, it makes you easier for them to control and you will always be trying to do better than you did before.

2. What are you motivated by? If you are motivated by the fear of not living up to the desired standards of the group or the leader the chances are very high that you have joined a group that is using mind control. You should be motivated by the purpose of the group such as saving the

endanger trees or whatever their purpose if you find that you are motivated by fear, you should leave the group immediately.

3. Is questioning the group or its leaders ideas generally frowned upon? If you are not allowed to state how you feel and express your own opinions, you have probably joined a group that is under the influence of mind control.

4. Does the group that you belong to feel that they are the only ones who have the true answers? Do they think that they were chosen or are above those who are not in the group? If the group you are in thinks that they have all the answers to life and only the members of the group are the ones who are able to understand what is really going on, you need to run as fast as you can because you are not only putting yourself in the position to be a victim of mind control, you are in the middle of a cult.

5. Do the members of the group behave as if they are robots? Sometimes this will

involve everyone dressing the same, wearing the same hair style, and can even be people acting exactly the same as everyone else. This is called group conformity and its sole purpose is to ensure that everyone act the same to ensure no one rebels.

6. Are you afraid to leave the group? If you find yourself in a situation where you belong to a group that you are afraid to leave because of whatever reason, you need to understand that sometimes those who use mind control, use fear as one of their techniques to control people. They may tell you that something terrible will happen to you if you leave the group because you are walking away from the truth. You have to understand this is just one of their mind control tactics and nothing bad is going to happen to you. On the other hand if you have been threatened with physical harm if you try to leave the group you do have the ability to contact local law enforcement and tell them what is going on. They will be able to remove you and help you find a safer location.

If you find that you are in a group that is using mind control on its members you have to find a way out. This may seem very difficult but you must remind yourself of all of the mental and emotional abuse that you will be subjected to if you continue to stay in such a group. You also have to understand that if you want out of the group, chances are there are others who also want out, it may just be that you taking the steps you need to take to remove this group from your life will show other members that it can be done and they can get their lives back.

Using mind control may have its benefits but when you find that you are the victim of mind control the benefits to the controller do not matter. Everyone has the right to think and act for themselves and to make the decisions that they feel are best for themselves. In this book I have given you many techniques that you can use in order to use mind control to benefit yourself but do not forget that you also need to be benefiting the subject at the same time. You don't want to be one of those people who continually take and take. If you use mind control to get something that you want, every now and then use mind control to give something back.

CHAPTER 7

Warnings About Using Mind Control

Using mind control on people obviously has some great benefits for the person who is in control. If the person who is in control is a caring person, mind control can have benefits for the subject as well, but there are some warnings you should understand before you decide to use mind control on anyone.

First you should understand that you could cause severe mental and psychological damage to the subject if you are not properly trained in using mind control techniques. This book was made to discuss several different techniques but without the proper training there is a great chance of causing permanent damage to your subject.

Another thing that can happen is that the controller may get caught up in using mind control on subjects and lose control themselves. This was briefly discussed in a previous chapter but I feel that it deserves a bit more discussion. When someone gets caught up in using mind control on others, we end up with evil cult leaders who cause groups of people to suffer at their hands.

Blocking out the subjects memories may allow them to get past some of their fears but it can also allow them to become fearless. This may cause the subject to put their life or the lives at others at risk.

Mind control may cause the subject to have severe panic attacks. This is especially true when the person is subjected to vivid imagery as a form of mind control and they are not used to such imagery.

If you use a trigger word in order to get the subject to comply they may hear the trigger word from someone else at a time when you do not want them to perform the action associated with the trigger word.

There are many things that could happen when you are using mind control on someone that could harm them or those around them, but given the fact that you are using mind control on them, the chances are that you really don't care how it could negatively affect them. What about how it could negatively affect you? If you are using mind control on people and it is found out, with enough evidence, you could be prosecuted. This is especially true if you caused them to bring harm to themselves or others, or if you caused them to give you all of their personal belongings. In court this is looked at the same as if you had walked in their house and stole everything they owned.

What will happen if people find out that you are using mind control? How will the people around you react? Chances are that they will feel whether it is true or not, that you have been using mind control on them as well. You will lose all of your friends and word will quickly get around that you have been using mind control on people. What would happen if your boss found out? He just gave you a huge raise and it comes to his attention that you are someone who uses mind control to get people to do what you want them to, I bet you lose that raise and possibly even your job even if you never used mind control on your boss at all.

Before you decide to use mind control, you have to look at all the possible outcomes. How would you feel if you caused permanent damage to one of your subjects? How would you react if those around you found out that you had the ability to use mind control on anyone you chose to? Is there a chance that you will become power hungry and turn into a vicious cult leader?

Some of these questions may seem farfetched but if you are truly considering using mind control on anyone than you must ask these types of questions. Deciding to use mind control is not a decision that should be made quickly nor should it be taken lightly. You have the knowledge that you need to control the mind of anyone in your life but the question that you should ask yourself is just because I can does it mean that I should?

If in fact you do decide to use mind control, I suggest that you start out small, use it for minor things in your life. If you find that you are able to control yourself and you do not become power hungry than you can move one to bigger things.

How will you know if you are becoming power hungry? You will know that you are becoming power hungry if you find that you are having the subject do things that could harm them. Or you will see that your subject seems to be miserable. You can also realize that you are only using mind control because you are power hungry if you find that you are never using your ability to use mind control to benefit your subject.

CONCLUSION

Thanks again for reading this book!

I do not have an opinion about where using mind control is right or wrong, but I do think that it can change your life if you decide to use it. Whether it changes your life for the better or for the worse is completely up to you and is in your control. You have to make sure you as a person are able to make the right choices when it comes to using mind control. Using mind control to make a sale, get your friend to exercise more often, or to help someone discover gifts that they never knew they had is fine. Using mind control to obtain followers and get them to do whatever you want while instilling fear in them, causing people to harm themselves or those around them, or taking everything you can get from your subject is wrong and I do not in any way endorse such behavior.

I wrote this book so people would understand how they can use mind control to benefit themselves and those around them in their daily lives. Not so people can harm their subjects and cause them to live in fear. I suggest that you take a good look at your motives before you use mind control and determine if it will help you become the person that you want to be. If you find that you want to use it to bring harm to others, I suggest you get some help and leave mind control alone. If you feel that you are a subject of mind control, please follow the advice given in this book to free yourself.

Thank you so much for taking the time for reading my book. I hope that it has helped you make the decision if you should use mind control or not and if you are a victim of mind control, I hope that it has helped you realize that you are.

Thank you,

Eleanor Price

PS. If you enjoyed this book, please help me out by kindly leaving a review!